THE DAN FOX PIANO LIBRARY

BIG-NOTE PIANO

# BEATLES big-note I

MW00446411

ARRANGED BY *Dan Fox*

## Contents

ISBN 0-7935-2280-3

HAL•LEONARD
CORPORATION
7777 W. BLUEMOUND RD. P.O. BOX 13819 MILWAUKEE, WI 53213

# AND I LOVE HER

Words and Music by
JOHN LENNON and PAUL McCARTNEY

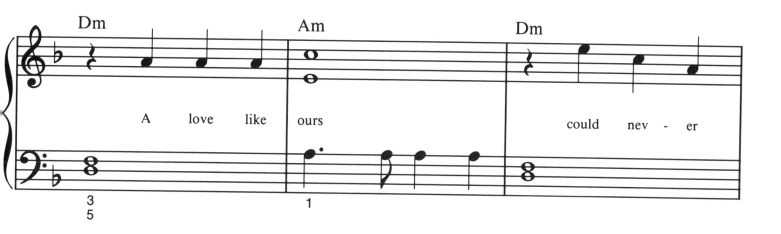

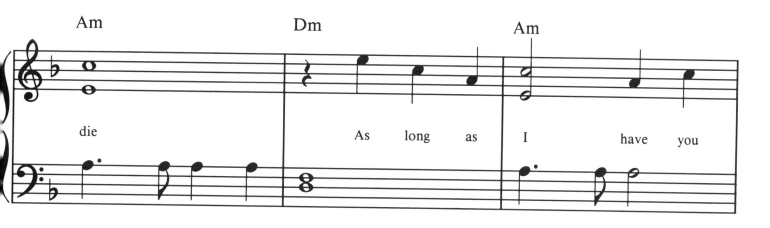

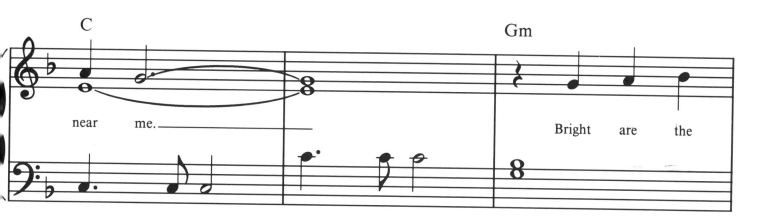

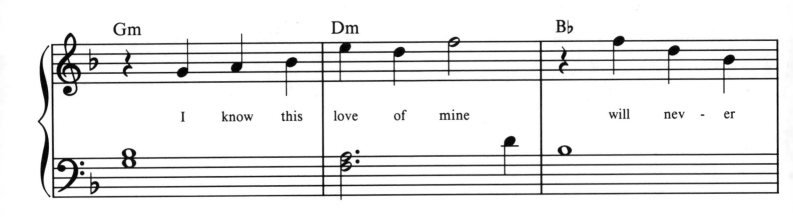

I know this love of mine will nev - er

die; \_\_\_\_\_ And I love her. \_\_\_\_\_

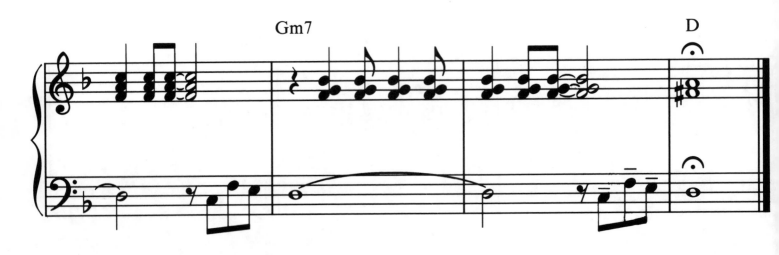

# EIGHT DAYS A WEEK

Words and Music by
JOHN LENNON and PAUL McCARTNEY

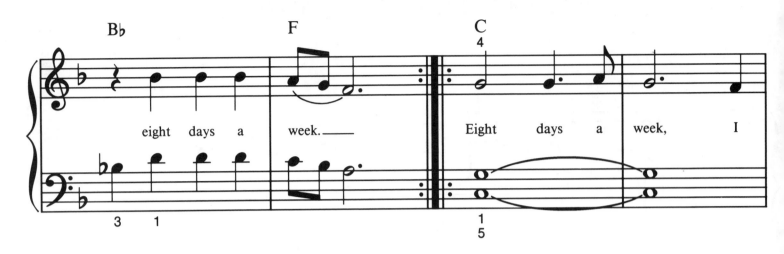

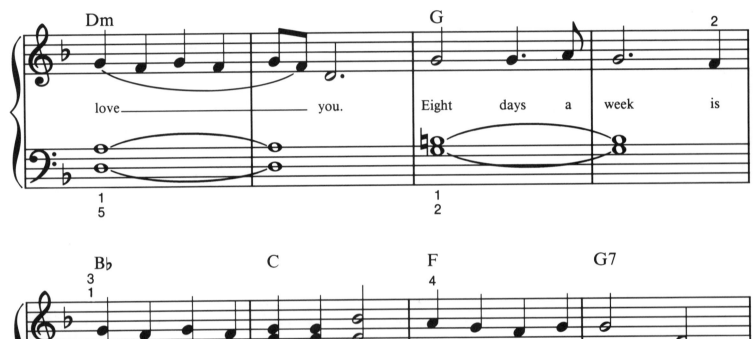

love,     babe,    just  like  I   need  you.}
say,      girl,    love  you  all the  time.}

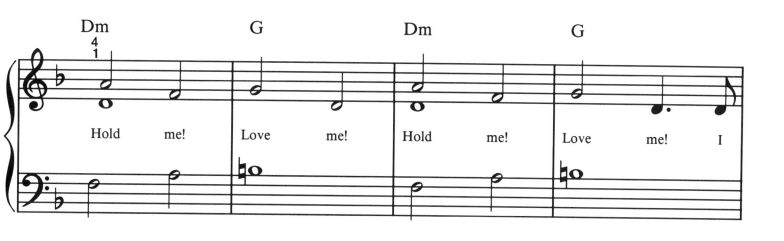

Hold  me!  Love  me!  Hold  me!  Love  me!  I

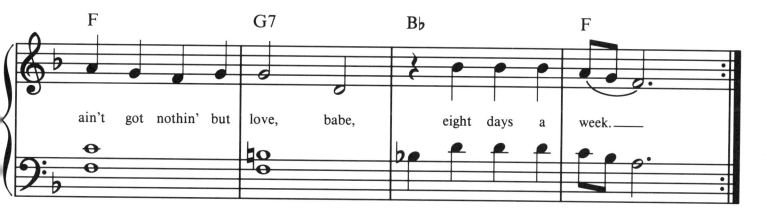

ain't  got nothin' but  love,  babe,  eight days  a  week.___

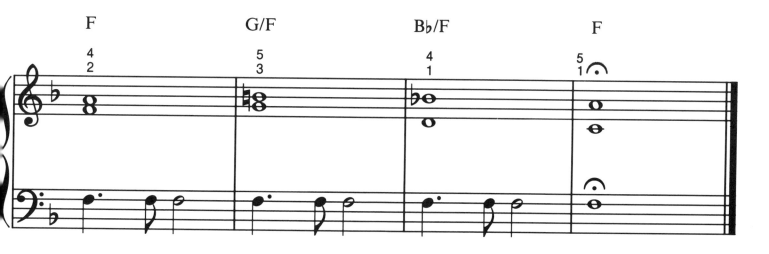

# BLACKBIRD

Words and Music by
JOHN LENNON and PAUL McCARTNEY

# ELEANOR RIGBY

Words and Music by
JOHN LENNON and PAUL McCARTNEY

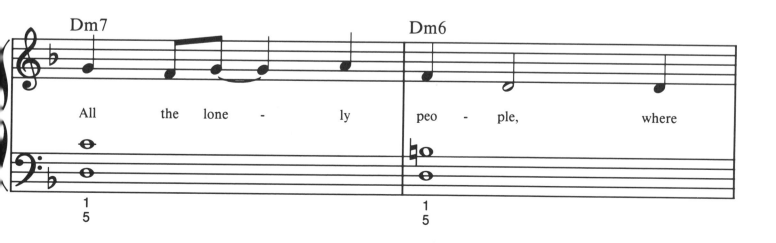

# GOOD DAY SUNSHINE

Words and Music by
JOHN LENNON and PAUL McCARTNEY

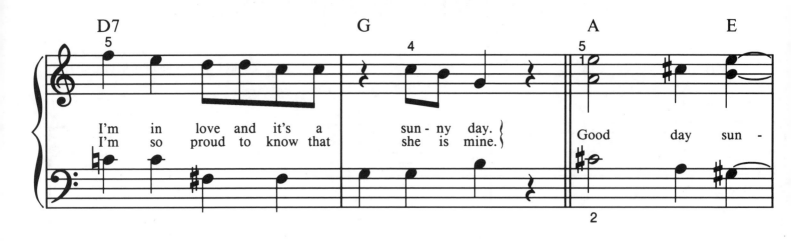

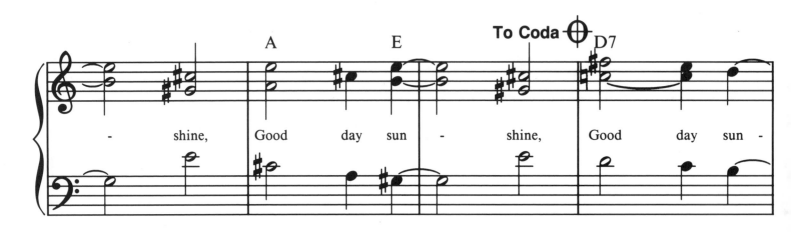

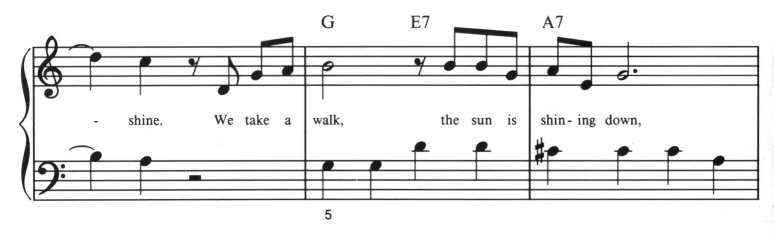

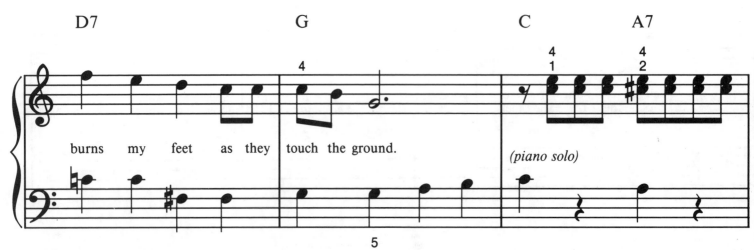

D.C. al Coda

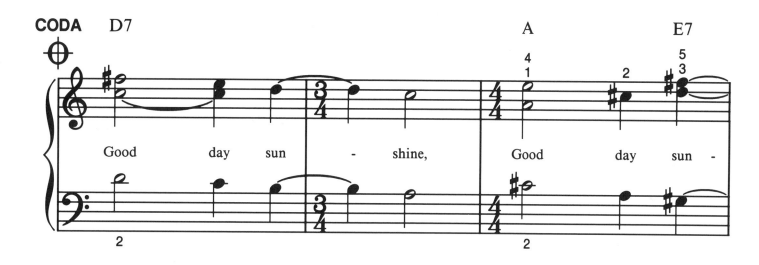

Good day sun - shine, Good day sun -

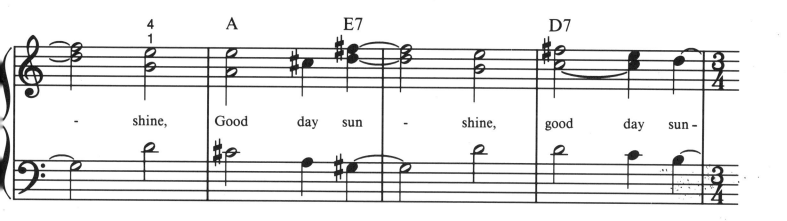

- shine, Good day sun - shine, good day sun -

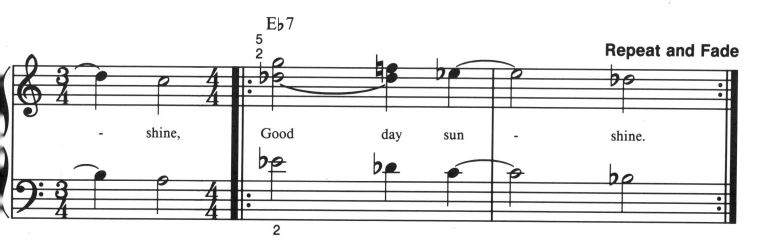

- shine, Good day sun - shine.

**Repeat and Fade**

# A HARD DAY'S NIGHT

Words and Music by
JOHN LENNON and PAUL McCARTNEY

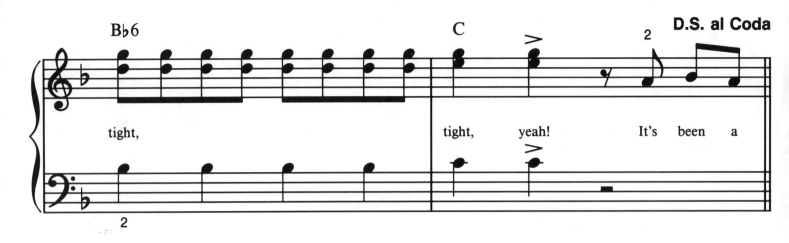

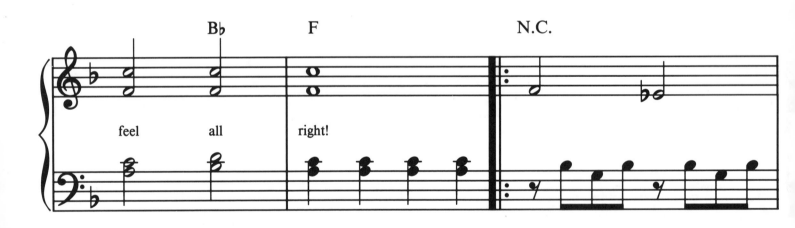

# IF I FELL

Words and Music by
JOHN LENNON and PAUL McCARTNEY

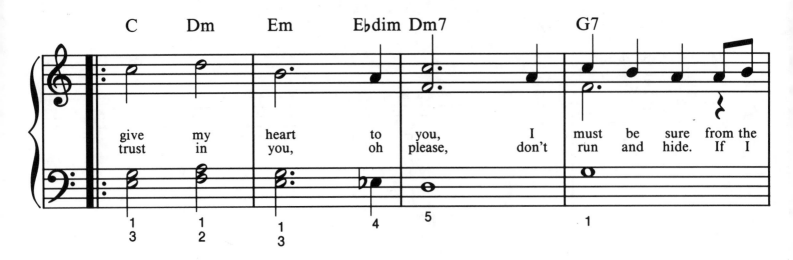

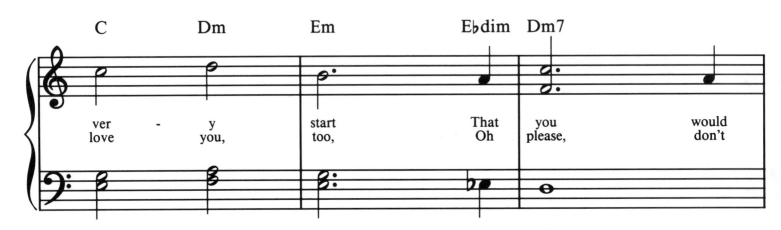

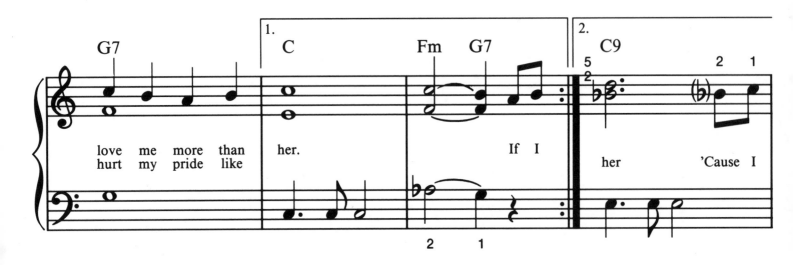

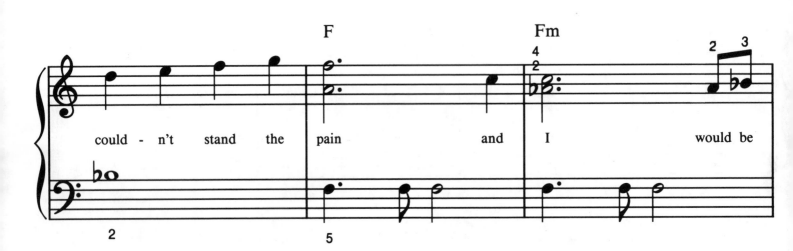

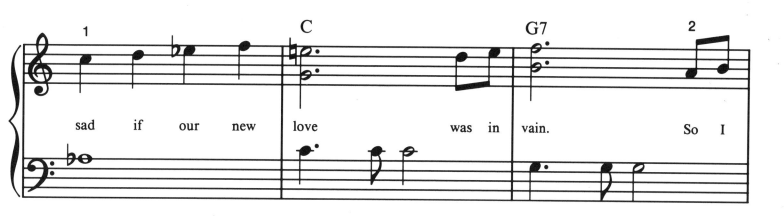

sad   if   our   new   love   was   in   vain.   So   I

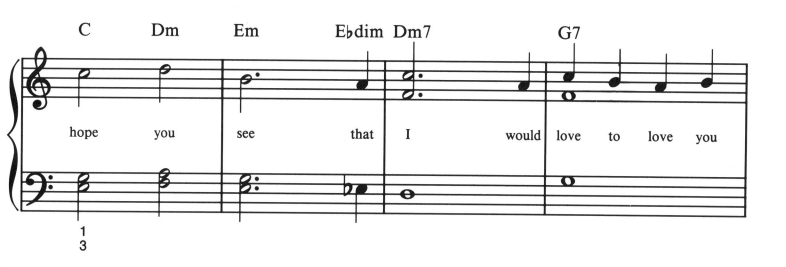

hope   you   see   that   I   would   love   to   love   you

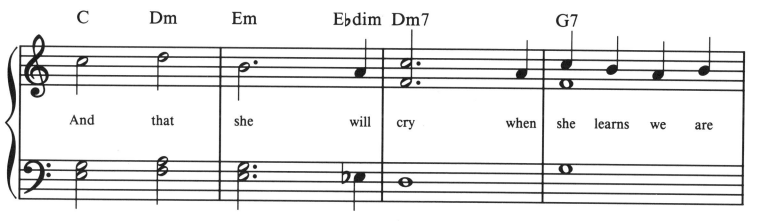

And   that   she   will   cry   when   she   learns   we   are

two,   if   I   fell   in   love   with   you.

5

# LET IT BE

Words and Music by
JOHN LENNON and PAUL McCARTNEY

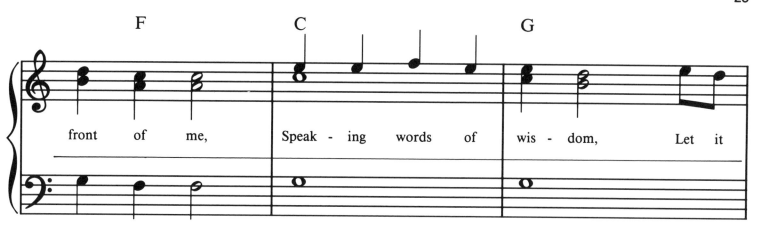

front of me, Speak - ing words of wis - dom, Let it

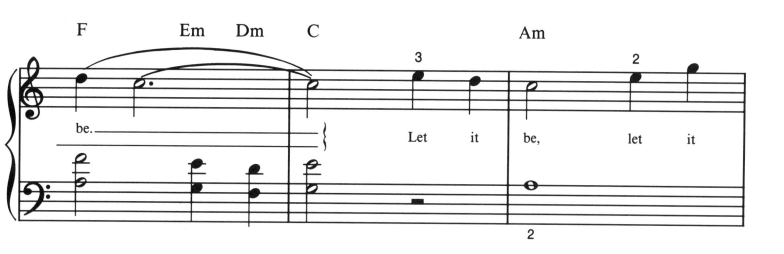

be. Let it be, let it

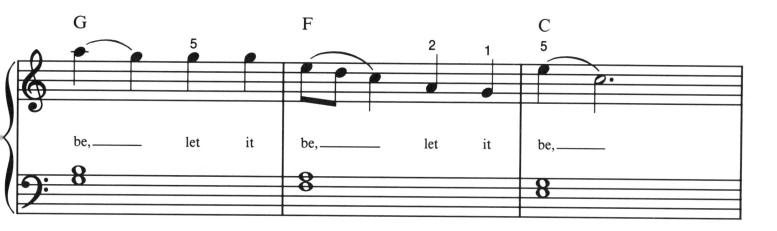

be, let it be, let it be,

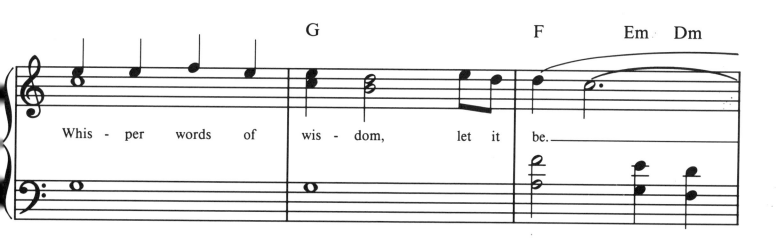

Whis - per words of wis - dom, let it be.

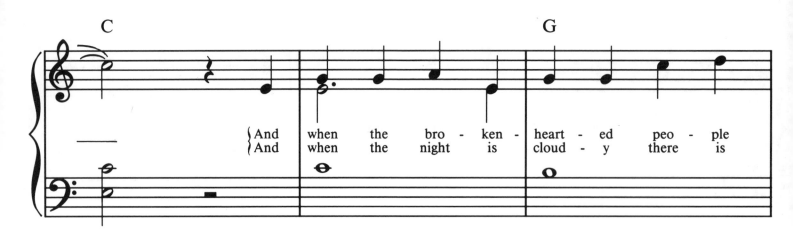

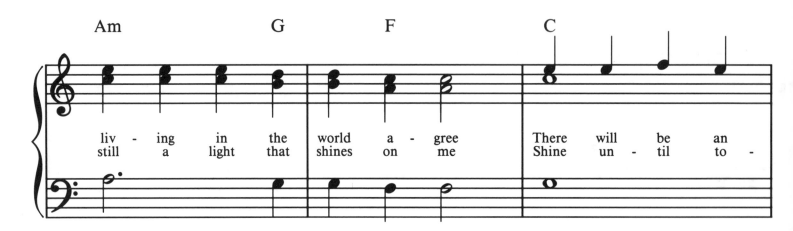

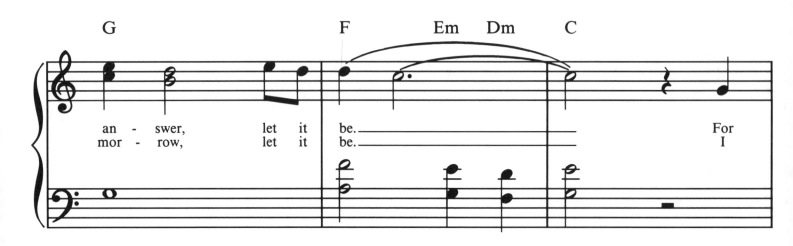

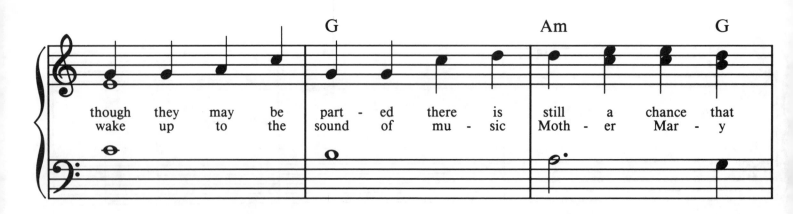

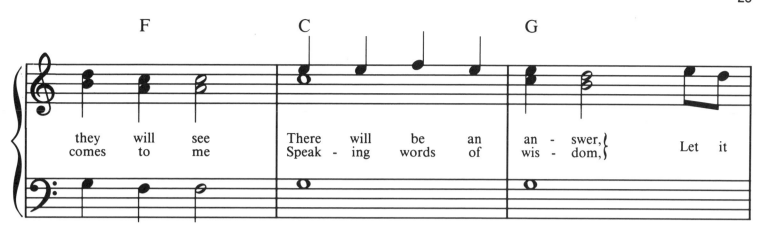

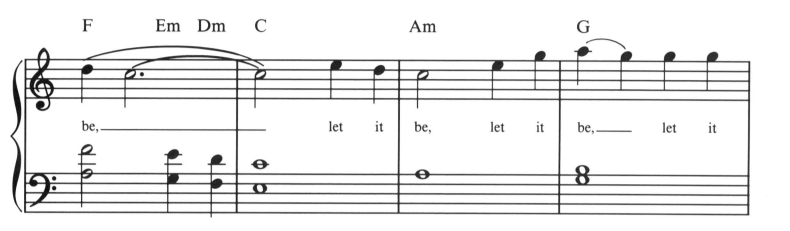

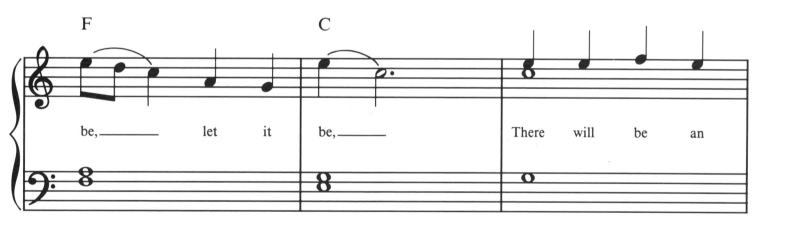

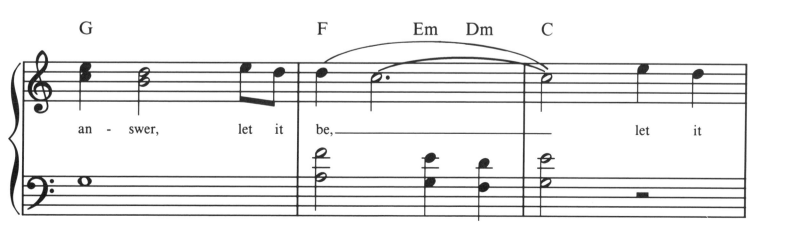

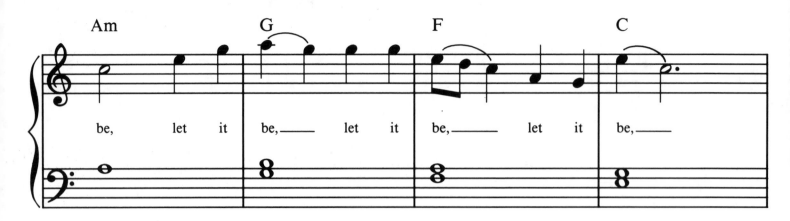

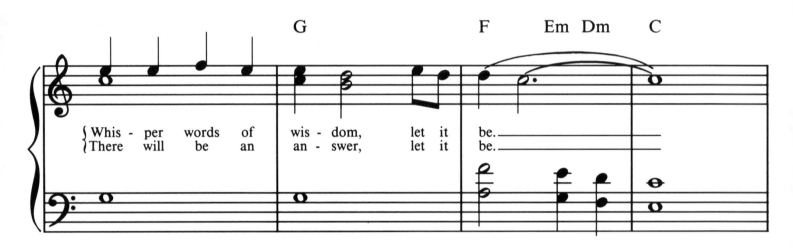

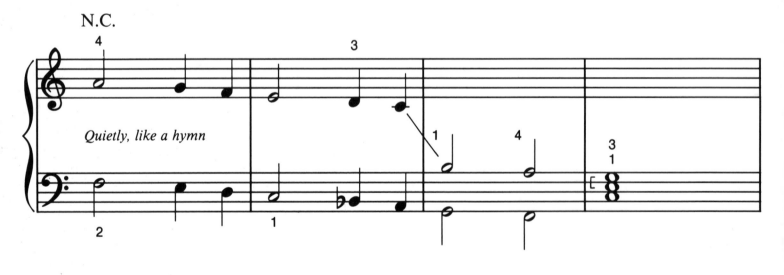

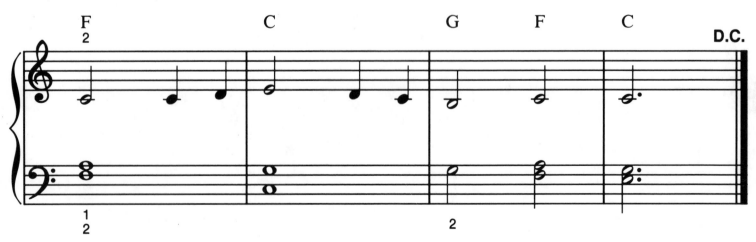

# NOWHERE MAN

Words and Music by
JOHN LENNON and PAUL McCARTNEY

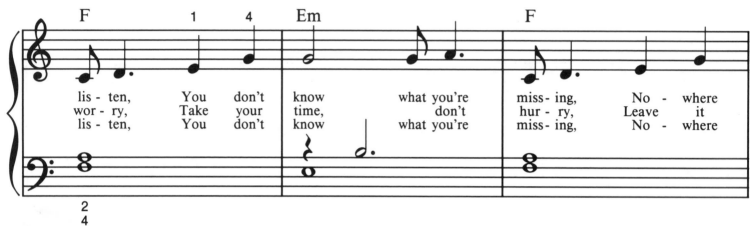

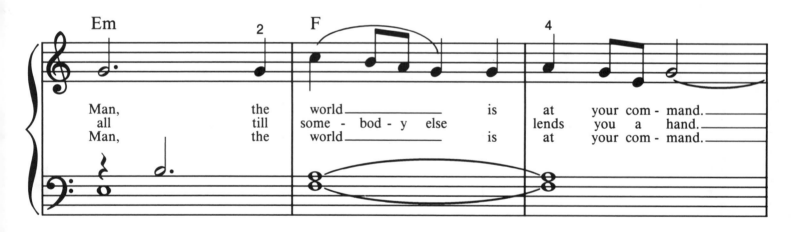

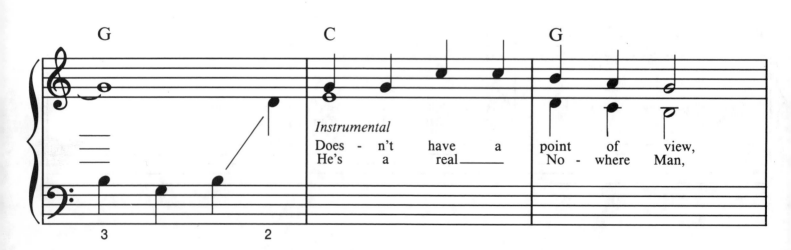

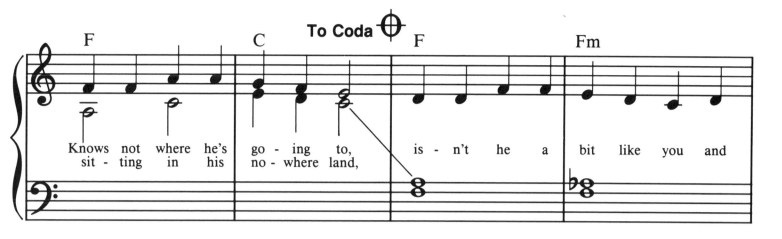

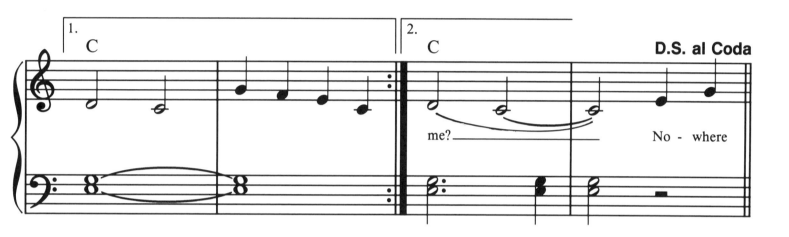

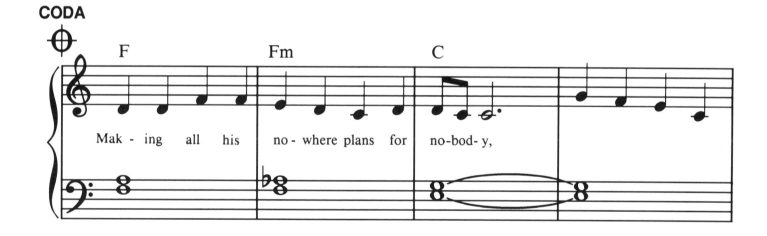

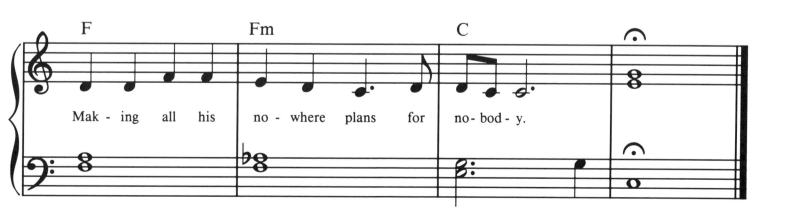

# OB-LA-DI, OB-LA-DA

Words and Music by
JOHN LENNON and PAUL McCARTNEY

Brightly, in 2 ( ♩ = 1 beat)

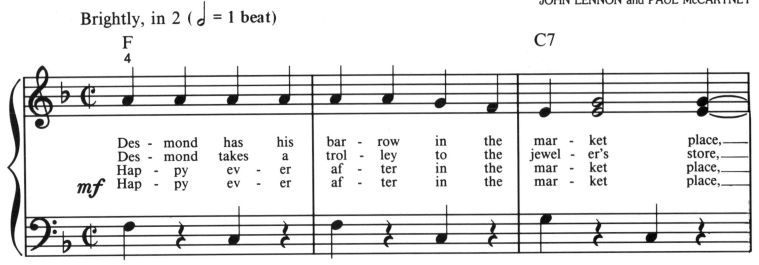

Des - mond has his bar - row in the mar - ket place,___
Des - mond takes a trol - ley to the jewel - er's store,___
Hap - py ev - er af - ter in the mar - ket place,___
Hap - py ev - er af - ter in the mar - ket place,___

Mol - ly is the sing - er in a
Buys a twen - ty car - at gold - en
Des - mond lets the chil - dren lend a
Mol - ly lets the chil - dren lend a

band.___
ring.___
hand,___
hand,___

Des - mond says to
Takes it back to
Mol - ly stays at
Des - mond stays at

Ob - la - di, ____ ob - la - da, ____ life goes on, ____ bra, ____

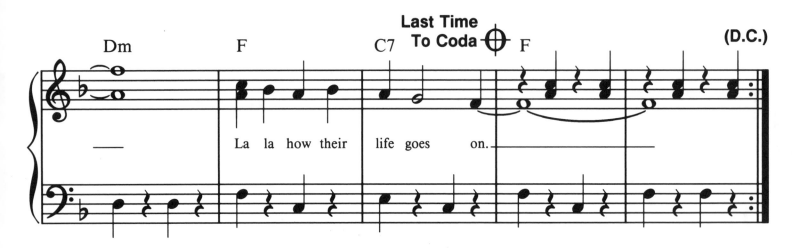

La la how their life goes on.

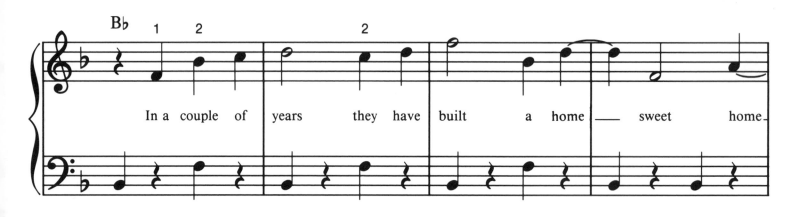

In a couple of years they have built a home ____ sweet home.

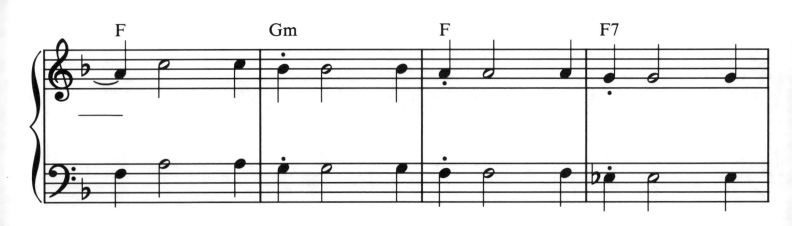

With a couple of kids run-ning in the yard___ of

**D.C.**
**(with repeats)**

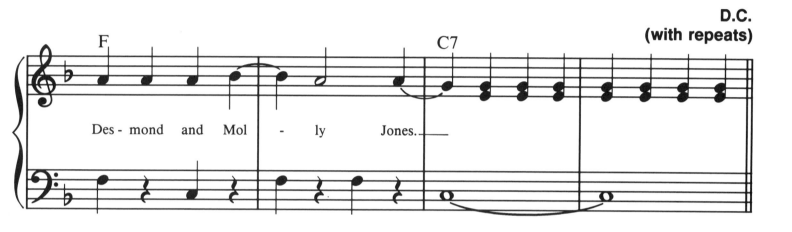

Des - mond and Mol - ly Jones.___

**CODA**

And if you want some fun

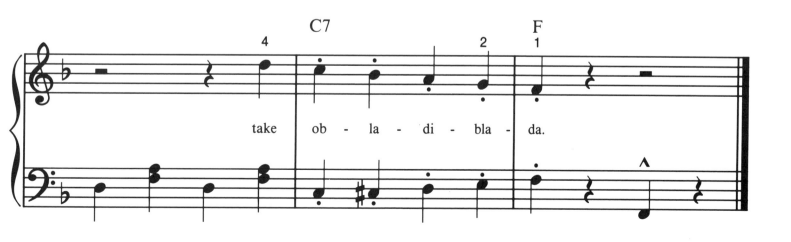

take ob - la - di - bla - da.

# SHE LOVES YOU

Words and Music by
JOHN LENNON and PAUL McCARTNEY

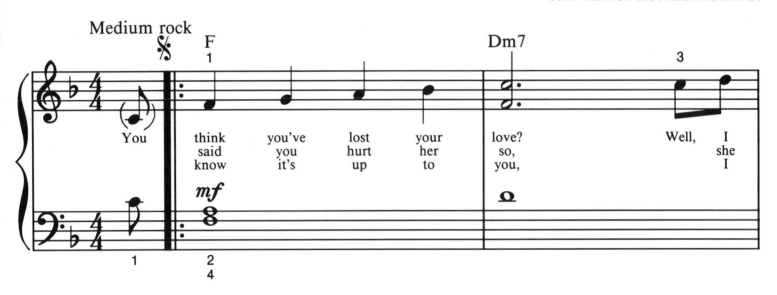

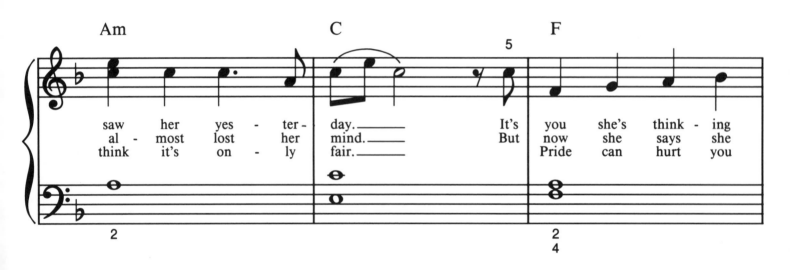

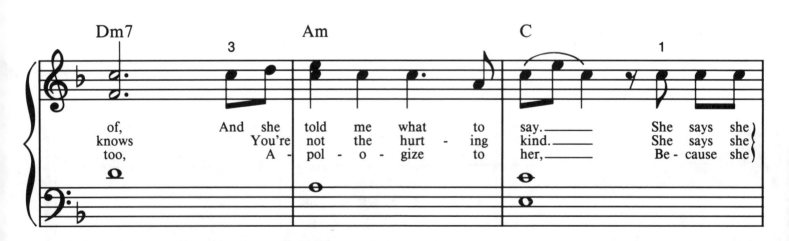

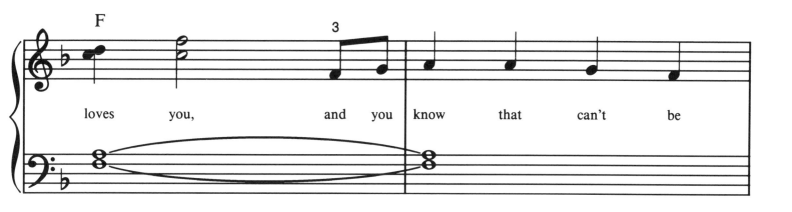

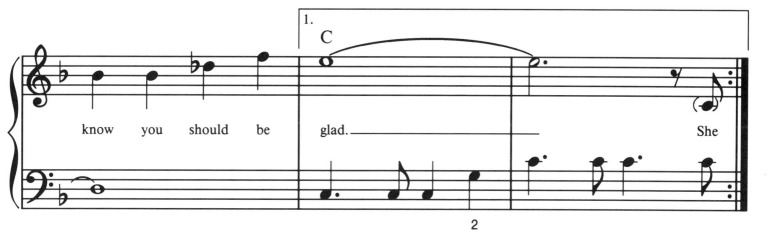

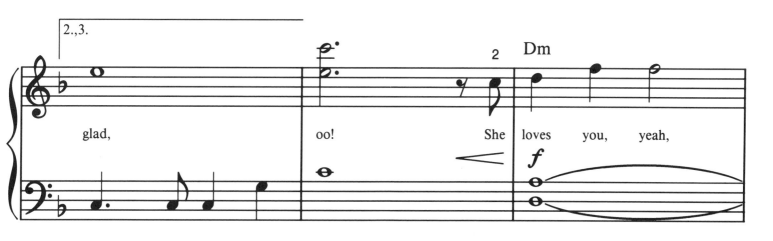

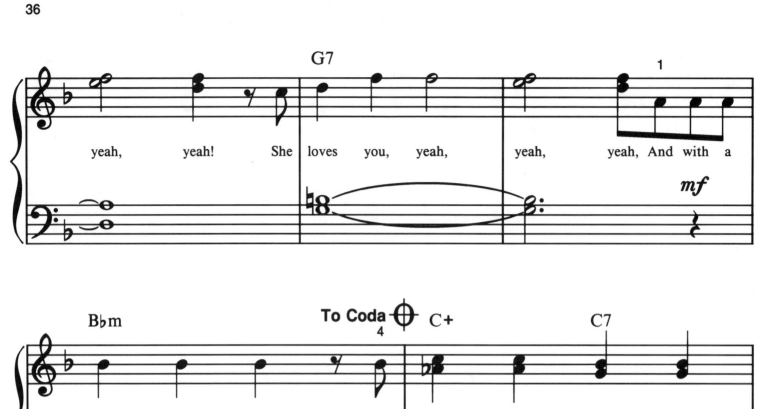

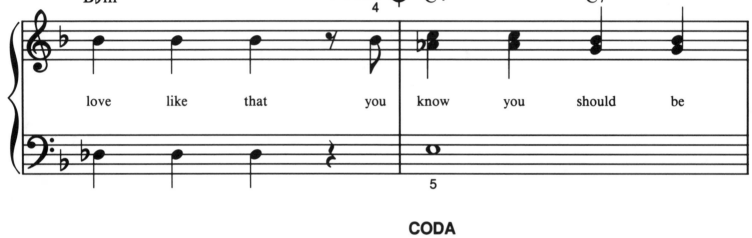

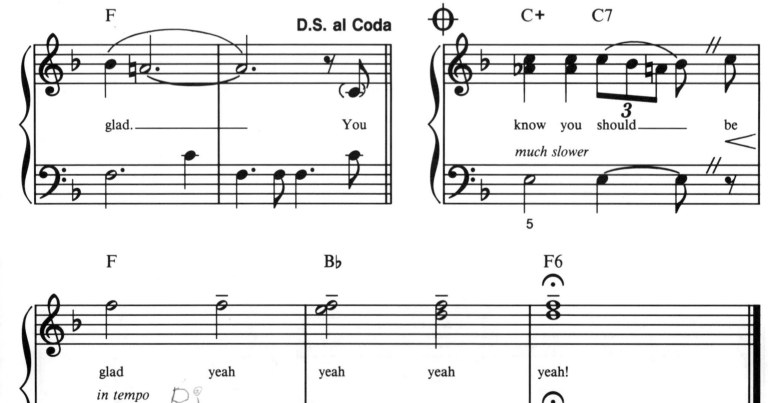

# WE CAN WORK IT OUT

Words and Music by
JOHN LENNON and PAUL McCARTNEY

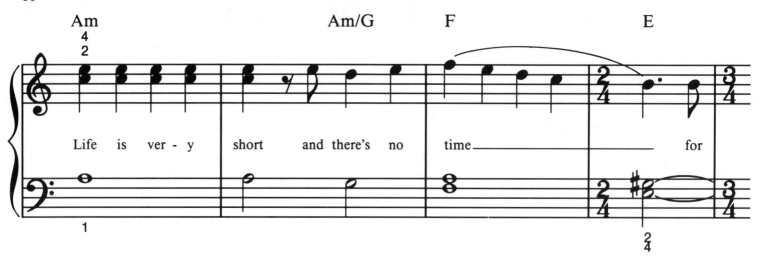

Life is ver - y short and there's no time_____ for

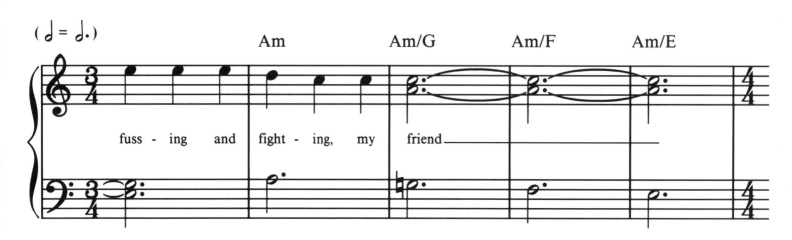

fuss - ing and fight - ing, my friend_____

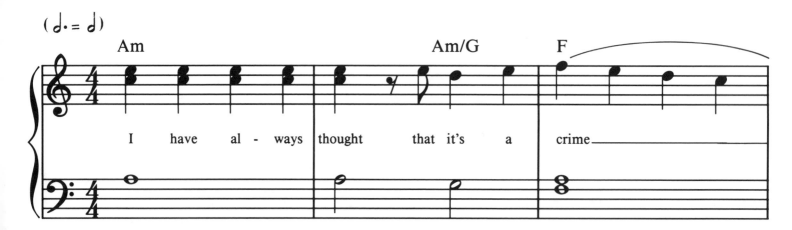

I have al - ways thought that it's a crime_____

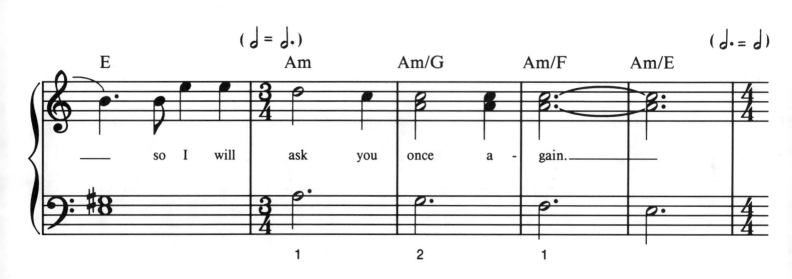

_____ so I will ask you once a - gain._____

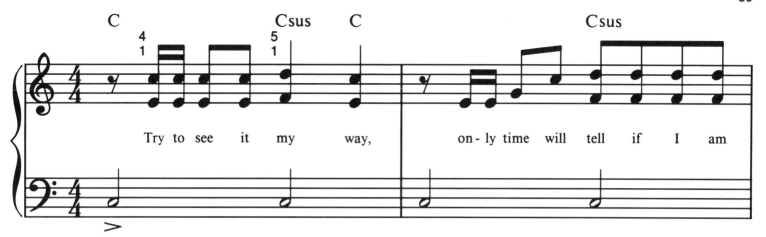

Try to see it my way, on-ly time will tell if I am

right or I am wrong. While you see it your way,

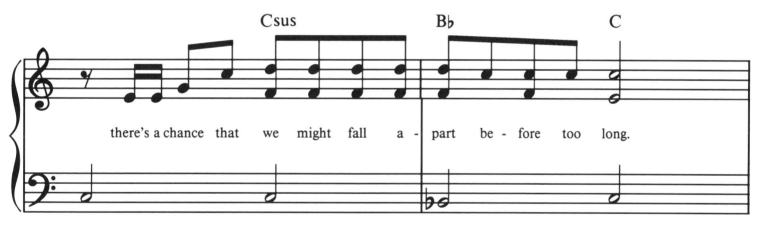

there's a chance that we might fall a - part be - fore too long.

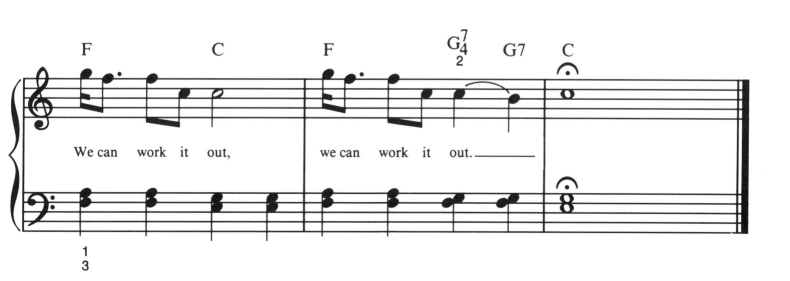

We can work it out, we can work it out._____

# TICKET TO RIDE

Words and Music by
JOHN LENNON and PAUL McCARTNEY

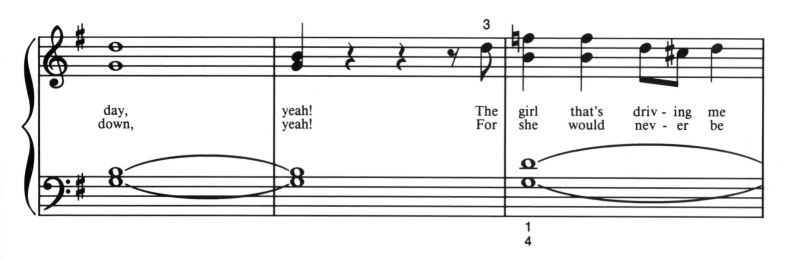

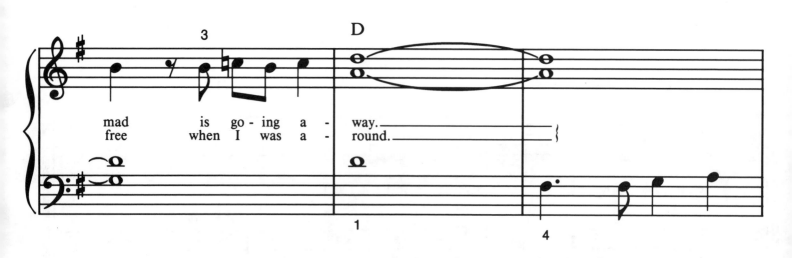

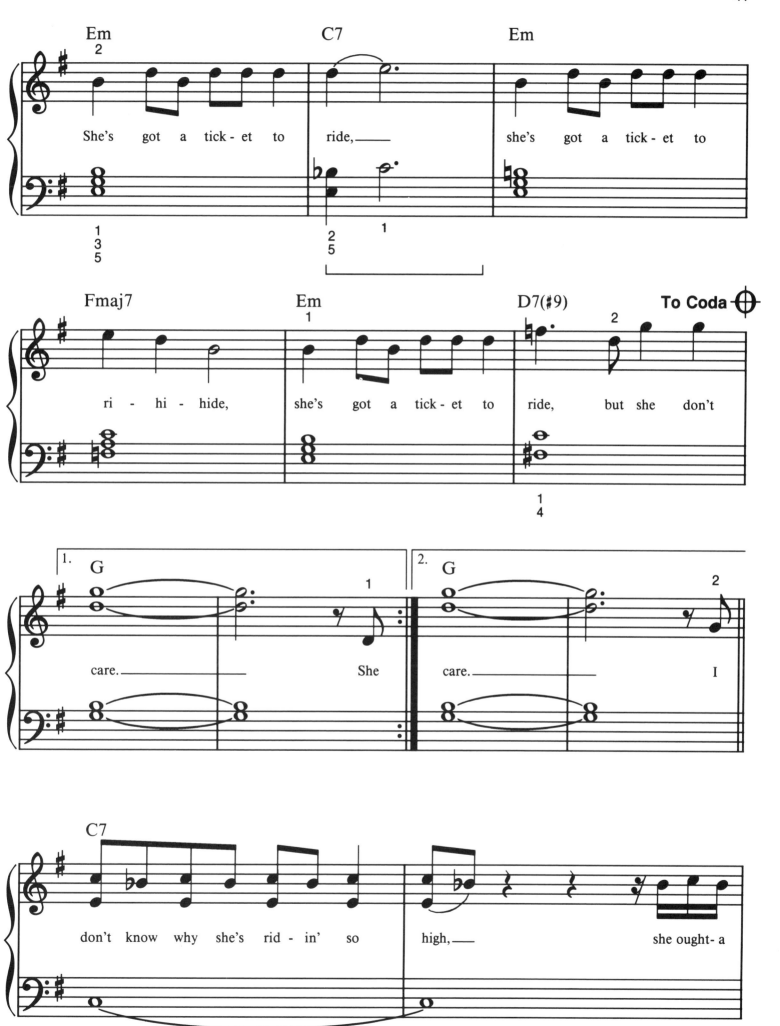

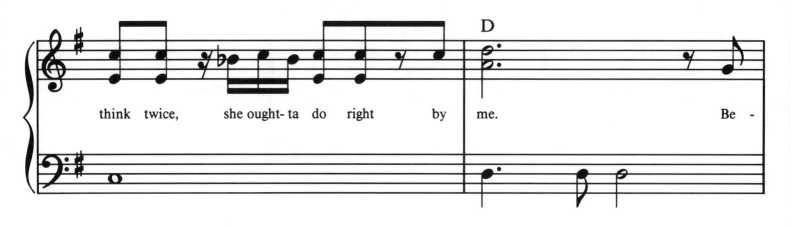

think twice, she ought-ta do right by me. Be -

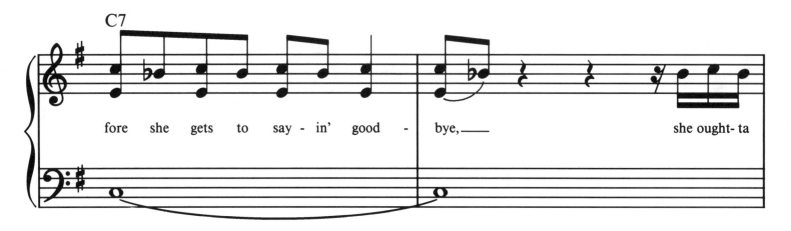

**C7**

fore she gets to say-in' good - bye,＿ she ought-ta

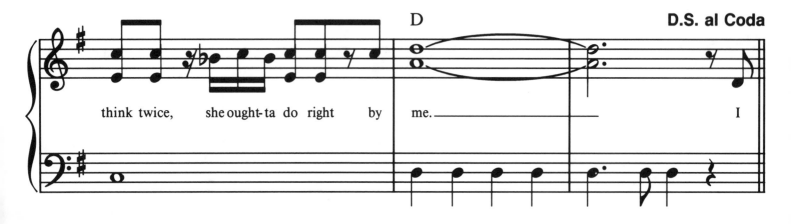

**D.S. al Coda**

think twice, she ought-ta do right by me.＿ I

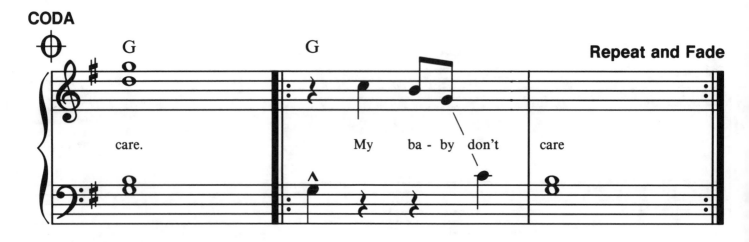

**CODA**

**Repeat and Fade**

care. My ba - by don't care

# You've Got To Hide Your Love Away

Words and Music by
JOHN LENNON and PAUL McCARTNEY

Moderately (each measure = 1 beat)

Here I stand head in
How I can e - ven

hand,_____ turn my face to the wall.
try,_____ I can_____ nev - er win

If she's gone, I can't go
Hear - ing them, see - ing

on_____ them,_____ two foot small._____
feel - ing in the state I'm in.

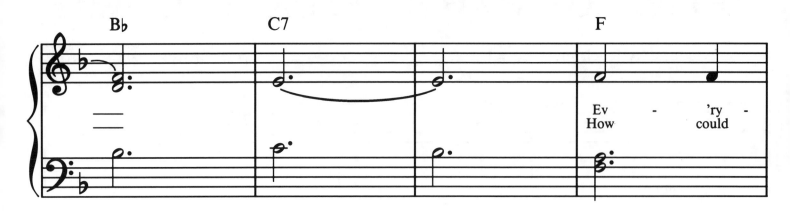

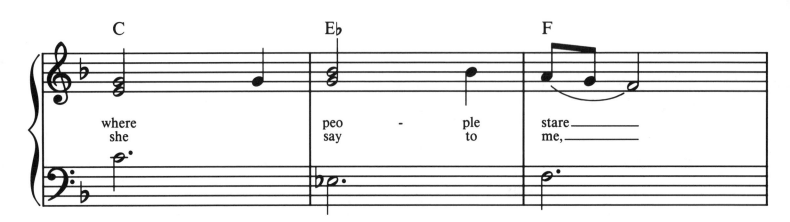

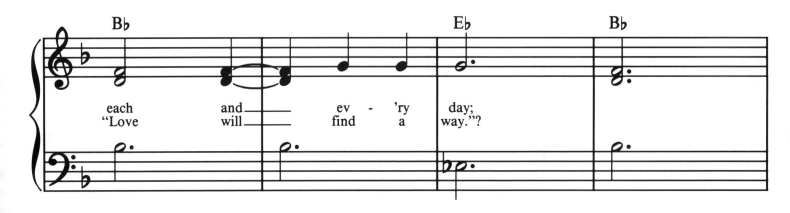

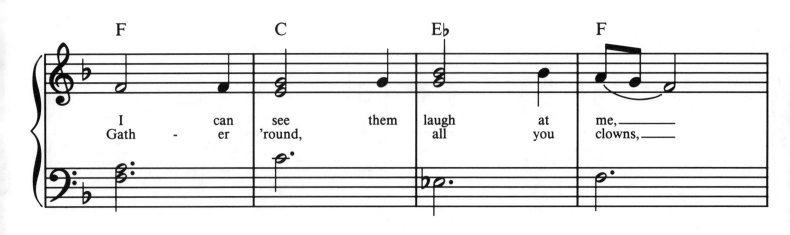

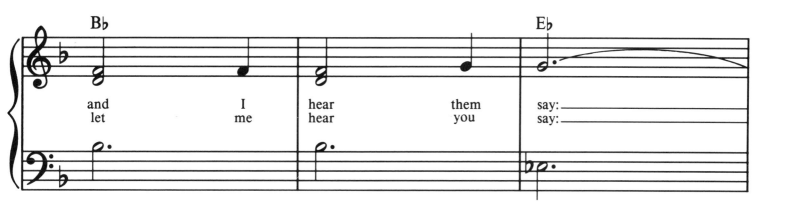

and       I     hear       them     say: _____
let      me     hear       you     say: _____

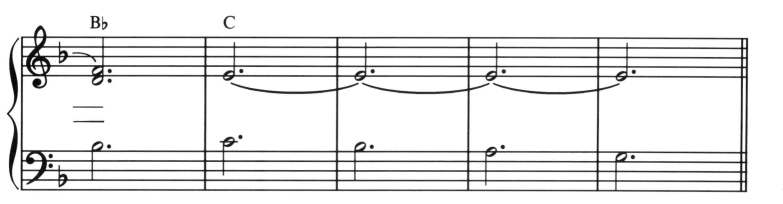

**Last time repeat chorus and fade**
**Chorus**

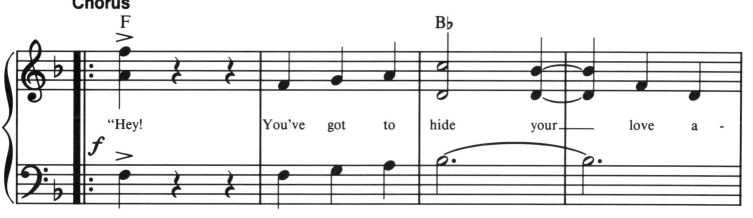

"Hey!      You've   got   to   hide    your ___ love a -

**After repeat, D.C.**

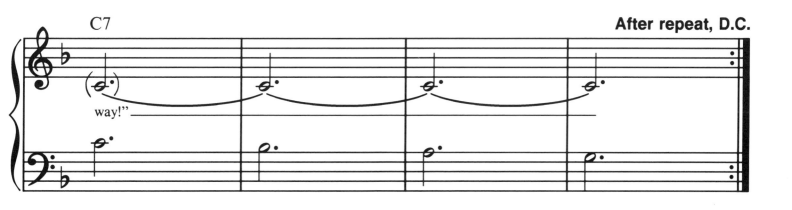

way!" _____

# TWIST AND SHOUT

Words and Music by
BERT RUSSELL and PHIL MEDLEY

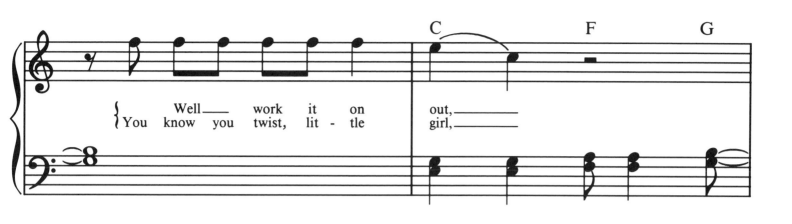

# WHEN I'M SIXTY FOUR

Words and Music by
JOHN LENNON and PAUL McCARTNEY

With an old-time beat ( ♩♩ = ♩.♪ )

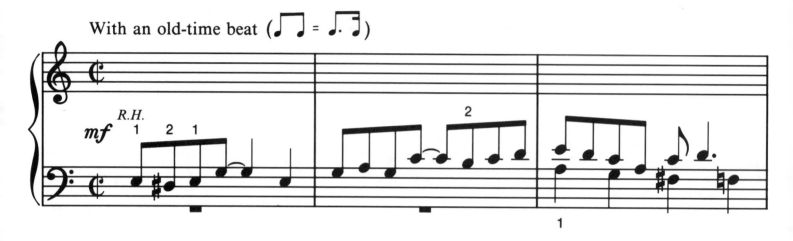

When I get old - er, losing my hair,—
I could be hand - y, mend - ing a fuse—
Send me a post - card, drop me a line—

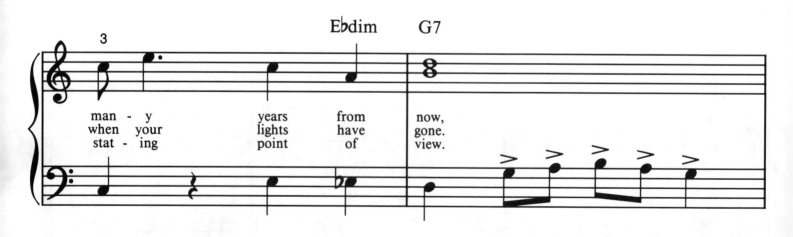

man - y years from now,
when your lights have gone.
stat - ing point of view.

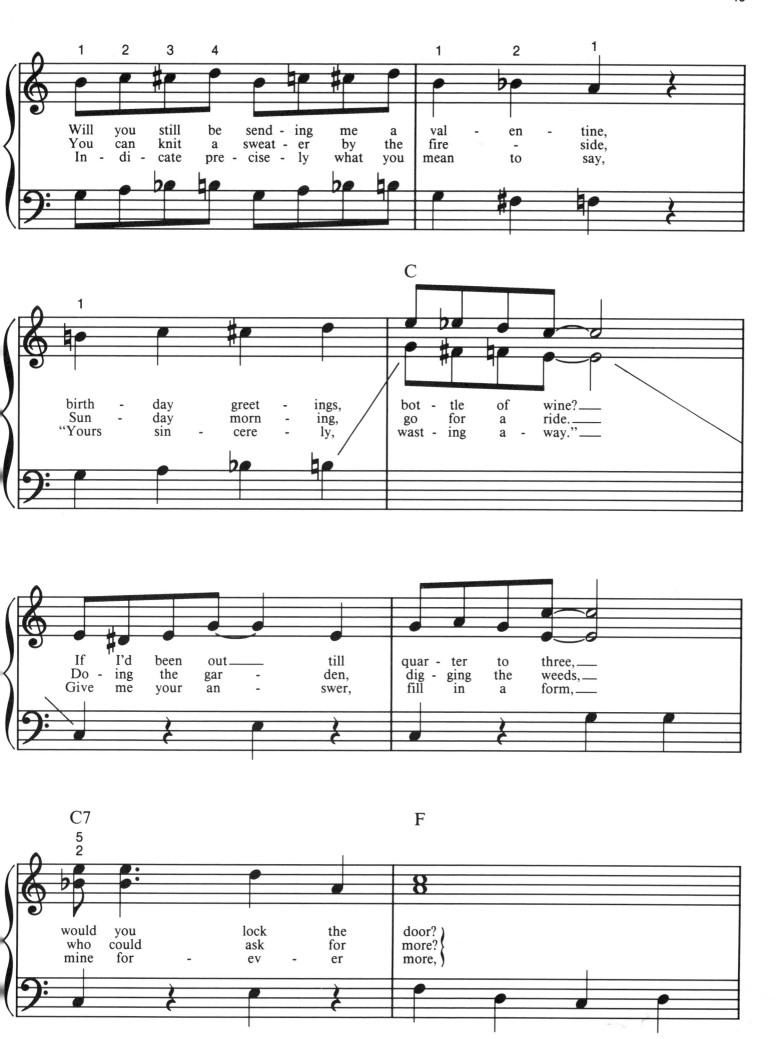

F#dim        C/G        A7

Will you still need ____ me, will you still feed ____ me,

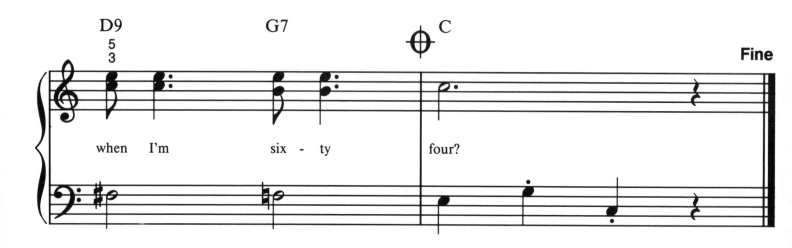

D9        G7        C        **Fine**

when I'm six - ty four?

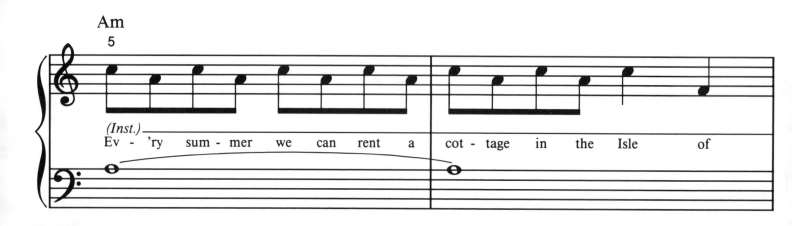

Am

*(Inst.)* ____
Ev - 'ry sum - mer we can rent a cot - tage in the Isle of

G        Am

Wight if it's not too dear.

You'll      be
We      shall

old - er too, _____
scrimp and save, _____

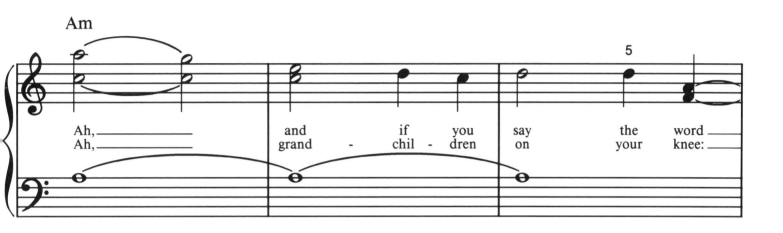

Ah, _____ and if you say the word _____
Ah, _____ grand - chil - dren on your knee: _____

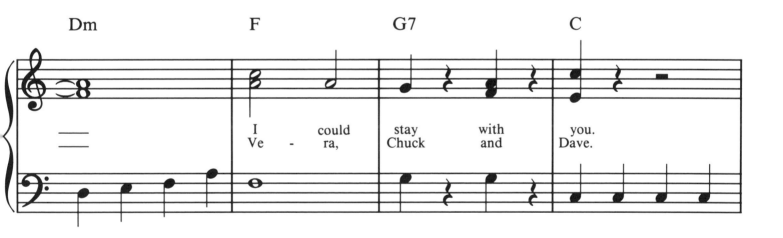

I could stay with you.
Ve - ra, Chuck and Dave.

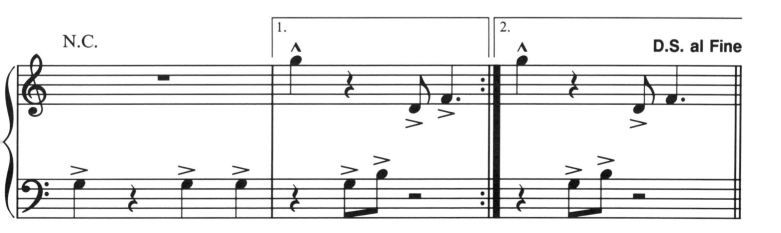

D.S. al Fine

# YELLOW SUBMARINE

Words and Music by
JOHN LENNON and PAUL McCARTNEY

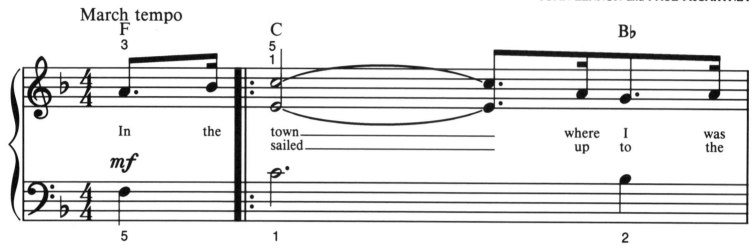

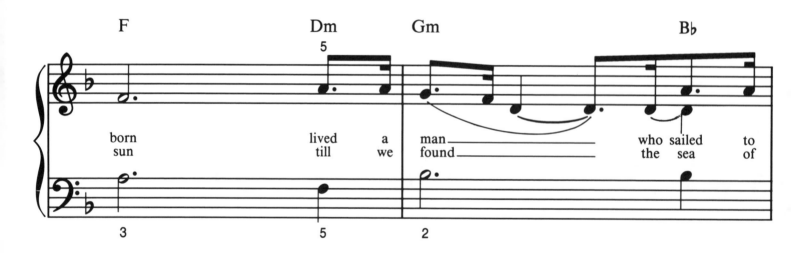

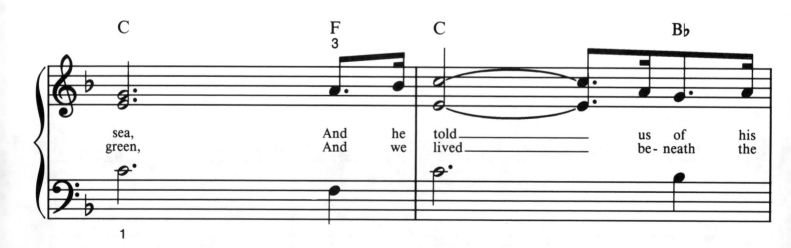

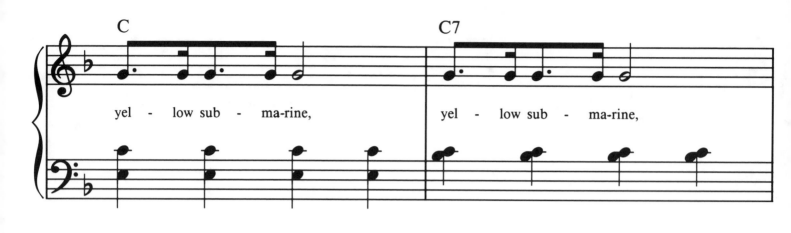

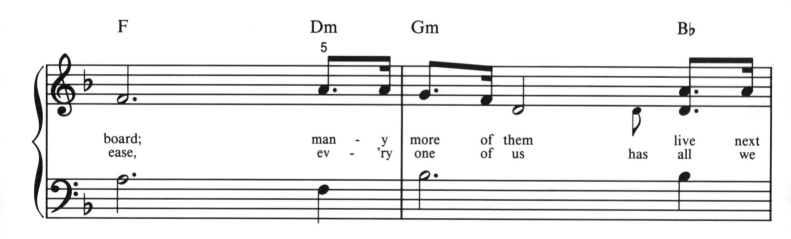

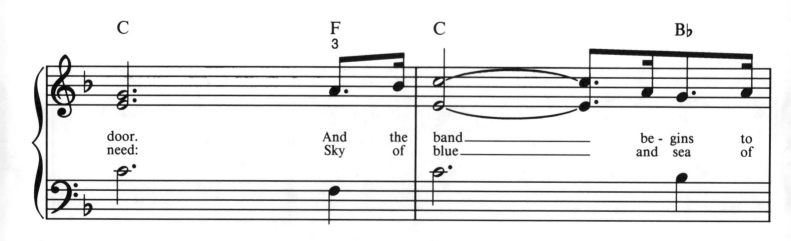

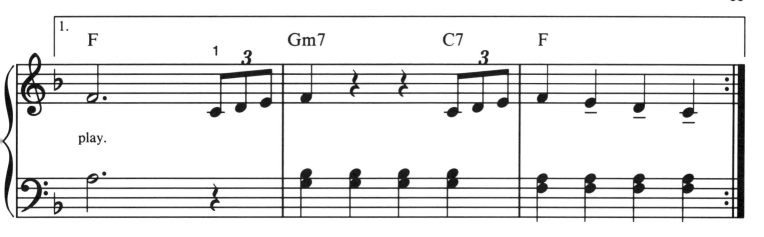

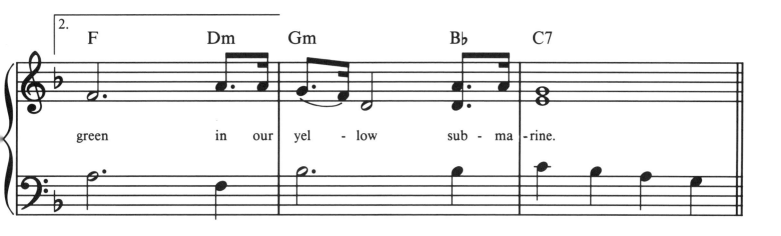

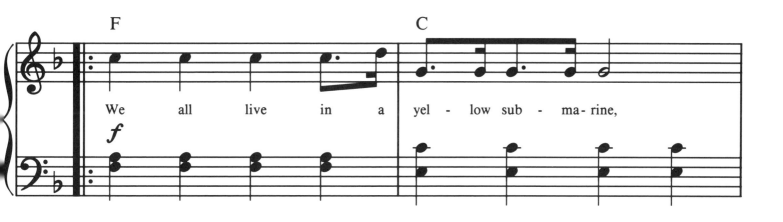

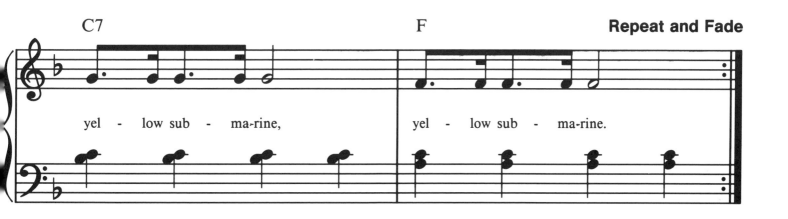

# THE BEST IN BIG-NOTE!

## More fun-filled collections from Hal Leonard Publishing

### BROADWAY CLASSICS
12 of the best songs from Broadway, including: Don't Cry For Me Argentina • Give My Regards To Broadway • Memory • Summertime • The Sound Of Music • and more.
00290180 .........................................................................................$7.95

### BROADWAY FAVORITES
More of the best of Broadway. 12 songs, including: Everything's Comin' Up Roses • I Dreamed A Dream • My Funny Valentine • Sunrise, Sunset.
00290184 .........................................................................................$7.95

### CONTEMPORARY FAVORITES
12 top hits, including: Don't Worry, Be Happy • Just The Way You Are • She's Like The Wind • Stand By Me • Under The Boardwalk • Yesterday • and more.
00290179 .........................................................................................$7.95

### FAVORITE CHILDREN'S SONGS
30 song to play and sing with children. Featuring: Peter Cottontail • Whistle A Happy Tune • It's A Small World • On The Good Ship Lollipop • The Rainbow Connection • and more.
00240251 .........................................................................................$5.95

### KERMIT'S FIRST RECITAL
10 classic melodies, including: Ave Maria • Clair De Lune • Ode To Joy • We Sail The Ocean Blue • more.
00240464 .........................................................................................$4.95

### MERRY CHRISTMAS
22 wonderful holiday melodies, including: The Chipmunk Song • Frosty The Snow Man • I'll Be Home For Christmas • Jingle-Bell Rock • Pretty Paper • Rudolph The Red-Nosed Reindeer • I Saw Mommy Kissing Santa Claus.
00240537 .........................................................................................$5.95

### TOP HITS
12 favorite hits, including: Can't Smile Without You • Candle In The Wind • I'll Always Love You • Kokomo • Lost In Your Eyes • Somewhere Out There • more.
00290181 .........................................................................................$7.95

### THE BIG BOOK OF CHILDREN'S SONGS
A collection of 55 favorites for children, including: Alouette • B-I-N-G-O • Bibbidi Bobbidi Boo • A Dream Is A Wish Your Heart Makes • I Whistle A Happy Tune • It's A Small World • London Bridge • Oh! Susanna • Old MacDonald Had A Farm • On Top Of Old Smoky • The Rainbow Connection • Supercalifragilisticexpialidocious • This Land Is Your Land • Twinkle, Twinkle Little Star • Yellow Submarine.
00290255 .........................................................................................$12.95

FOR MORE INFORMATION, SEE YOUR LOCAL MUSIC DEALER, OR WRITE TO:

Prices, content and availability subject to change without notice. Certain products may not be available outside of the U.S.A.

0292

## HAL•LEONARD™
### CORPORATION
7777 W. BLUEMOUND RD. P.O. BOX 13819 MILWAUKEE, WI 53213